Read, Search & Find®

Kidsbooks®

Illustrations Copyright © 2012 Orpheus Books Ltd
2 Church Green Witney, Oxon OX28 4AW

Illustrated by Peter Dennis (Linda Rogers Associates)
Written by Raphael Rosen

Text and Design Copyright © 2012 Kidsbooks, LLC.
Read, Search & Find is a registered trademark of Kidsbooks, LLC.
3535 West Peterson Avenue
Chicago, IL 60659

Printed in China
121201001SZ

Visit us at www.kidsbooks.com®

Contents

Introduction

When you look into the night sky,
what do you see? In the great open space,
a fascinating world beyond Earth awaits!

SPACE will take you into the final frontier to
learn all about our solar system and our universe.
It may seem like the Earth is pretty big, but it's just
a tiny part of a much bigger puzzle! Search & find®
activities will introduce you to the kinds of tools
and equipment astronauts use, planets and
moons within our solar system, and even
some faraway galaxies and stars.

Blast off into the **Find Out More** section in the
back of this book to unlock even more mysteries
of the universe where we live.

So take one small step for man and
Read, Search & Find® all about the
wonders of space!

Night Sky

At night, you can see thousands of stars in the sky. They are many millions of miles away and are made of hot gas that shines for billions of years. Sometimes you can see planets and moons in the night sky, too. They are much closer to Earth than the stars. If you use a telescope, you can see details of these planets and moons.

Search & find the following items.

Star
Stars are very large—much larger than planets. Our Sun is a star, and one million Earths could fit inside it.

Comet Tail
Comets are actually just balls of mushy ice and dust.

Find Out More
on page 26

6

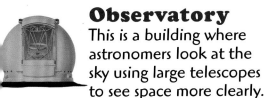

Observatory
This is a building where astronomers look at the sky using large telescopes to see space more clearly.

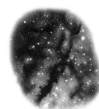

Milky Way
The Milky Way looks like a smear of white, but it is really a galaxy made up of hundreds of billions of stars.

Mare
A mare [MAHR-ay] is a large area of flat ground on the Moon. When astronauts first landed on the Moon, they went to a mare.

Orion Constellation
Some ancient cultures believed that this group of stars looked like a hunter from Greek mythology named Orion.

Shooting Star
A shooting star is not a star at all, but a rock called a meteor that falls from space into Earth's atmosphere. It either burns up or lands on Earth's surface.

Telescope
This scientific instrument for studying the skies was first made popular by Galileo Galilei, who lived in the 1600s.

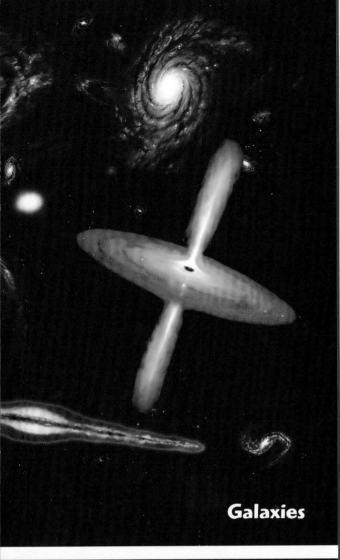

Galaxies

Stars

Galaxies and Stars

Galaxies are collections of billions of stars. They have many shapes—our own Milky Way Galaxy is shaped like a spiral. The centers of most galaxies have black holes, which are the cores of giant stars that have collapsed. The stars within galaxies come in many sizes. Large, cool stars are called red giants. Smaller stars at the end of their life spans are called white dwarfs. Stars form from giant clouds of gas called nebulae [NEB-you-lee].

Search & find the following items.

Nebula
This is a large blob of gas floating in space. Sometimes, if the nebula is dense enough, the gas condenses to form a star.

Supernova
When a large star reaches the end of its life, it explodes. The explosion is called a supernova.

Red Giant
A red giant is so large that if one were where the Sun is now, the Earth would be *inside* the red giant!

White Dwarf
These are small and very dense stars created when an old star sheds its outer gas layers.

Black Hole Jet
A black hole is a very dense object created when a large star collapses. When matter falls into a black hole, a jet of microscopic particles shoots out at very high speed.

Spiral Galaxy
Spiral galaxies are very common. They have a central bulge where a large number of stars are tightly packed, and arms that radiate from the center.

Galaxy Arm
In spiral galaxies, the arms are large collections of stars that branch off from the center. New stars are born in the arms.

Find Out More on page 27

9

Solar System

Our solar system is made up of a star (the Sun), eight planets (Mercury, Venus, Earth, Mars, Jupiter, Saturn, Uranus, and Neptune), asteroids, and a lot of gas and dust. Each planet moves around the Sun in an egg-shaped path called an orbit. Planets also orbit other stars in other solar systems in our galaxy.

Search & find these celestial bodies.

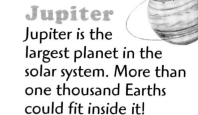

Jupiter

Jupiter is the largest planet in the solar system. More than one thousand Earths could fit inside it!

Sun

The Sun's light and heat make life on Earth possible. The Sun is 93 million miles away from Earth.

Venus

This planet is almost the same size as Earth but is covered with clouds that trap heat, so it's much hotter than Earth.

Neptune

This planet is so far from the Sun that one orbit takes 165 years. It has a large visible storm called the Great Dark Spot.

Uranus

Uranus was discovered in 1781. It's turned sideways on its axis, so it rotates on its side!

Saturn

This is the second largest planet in the solar system, is known for its beautiful rings made of ice, rocks, and dust.

Pluto

Pluto used to be considered a ninth planet. But astronomers renamed it a dwarf planet in 2006.

Find Out More
on page 27

Planets and Moons

Our solar system has eight planets. Some of those planets are made of rock, and others are made of gas. Most of the planets have moons. A moon is a large body, not man-made, that orbits a planet.

Search & find the following items.

Titan

Titan is the biggest of the fifty-three moons that orbit Saturn. It is covered with thick clouds.

Europa

Europa [yur-O-pah] orbits Jupiter, and its surface is covered with ice. Scientists believe that life may exist on Europa.

Ganymede

Ganymede [GAN-ee-meed] also orbits Jupiter. It is the solar system's largest moon, bigger than both Mercury and Pluto.

Phobos

Phobos [FOH-bohs] one of the moons of Mars, races around Mars three times a day, and has a crater 6 miles wide.

Io

Io is one of Jupiter's moons. Its surface is filled with volcanoes and pools of lava.

Mercury

This is the closest planet to the Sun. Its surface can be very hot—up to 800° Fahrenheit!

Mars Ice Caps

Just like Earth, the planet Mars has ice at its north and south poles.

Earth

Earth is the third planet from the Sun. It's where we all live, and the only planet we know of that has life on it.

Asteroid Belt

Asteroids are rocks that travel through space. The asteroid belt is a collection of asteroids between Mars and Jupiter.

Find Out More
on page 28

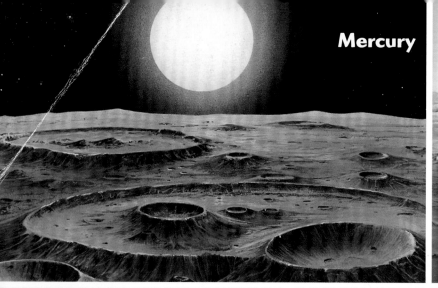
Mercury

Venus

Mars

Io

Miranda

Triton

Moon Rock

Humans first visited the Moon in 1969.
They brought back rocks so scientists
could study them.
Moon rocks are
billions of years old.

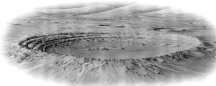

Atmosphere

Atmosphere is the air around
a planet. Titan's atmosphere
is thick and smoggy, with an
orange color.

Moon

Titan

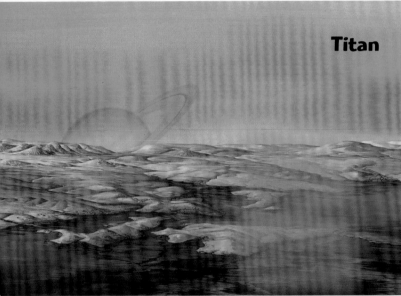

Pluto

Space Landscapes

The surfaces of the solar system's planets and moons come in a huge variety. Some are icy, some are hot. Some are flat and barren, and some have tall mountains. The surfaces are often shaped by meteor collisions and volcanic eruptions, and also by the gravitational pull of other bodies around them.

Search & find the following items.

Find Out More on page 28

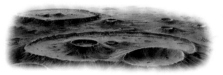

Crater
This is a pit where an asteroid hit a planet or moon. Some of Earth's biggest craters are more than 150 miles across!

Lava
Lava is rock from deep inside a planet or moon that is so hot, it flows like a liquid.

Geyser
Geysers [GAI-zers] spew liquid and gas into the atmosphere. Some geysers on Io shoot liquid 50 miles into the air!

Cliffs
Miranda, one of Uranus's moons, has deep valleys and high cliffs. Some valleys are deeper than the Grand Canyon!

Volcano
Triton, one of Neptune's moons, has volcanoes that resemble smokestacks. Instead of lava, these volcanoes shoot out dust, water, and nitrogen.

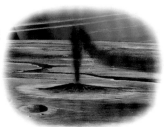

15

Spacecraft

There are many kinds of spacecraft. Some help people transmit information, like phone calls and television. Others take people to the Moon. People have been sending spacecraft into outer space for many years.

Search & find the following objects.

Satellite
A satellite is any man-made object that orbits the Earth. The first satellite was Sputnik, launched by the Soviet Union in 1957.

Voyager
Voyagers 1 and 2 were space probes launched in the 1970s to explore Jupiter and Saturn. They are now so far away that they have left our solar system!

Gemini 7
This spacecraft held two astronauts and stayed in orbit for almost two weeks in 1965.

Hubble Space Telescope
This telescope orbits the Earth and takes extremely good pictures of faraway stars and galaxies.

Magellan
This craft was sent to take pictures of Venus. It was the first spacecraft to be launched from the Space Shuttle.

Solar Panels
These convert light into electricity. They help power satellites, space telescopes, and space stations.

Space Shuttle
This manned craft has wings so it can land like an airplane. It can be used over and over again.

Antenna
Scientists control spacecraft by sending commands to the spacecrafts' antennas. Antennas can also send information back to Earth.

Find Out More on page 29

Space Shuttle

The Space Shuttle was the first manned spacecraft that could be used again and again. It had a 60-foot-long payload bay (a space where cargo could be packed) that could carry satellites and other equipment into orbit. There have been six Space Shuttles: Enterprise, Columbia, Challenger, Discovery, Atlantis, and Endeavour.

Search & find the items below.

Booster Rocket
The Space Shuttle rides into space on one fuel tank and two booster rockets. After the shuttle reaches space, the rockets detach and fall into the ocean.

Landing Gear
When the Space Shuttle's mission is over, it returns to Earth and lands on wheels like those found on an airplane.

Wing Flap
By adjusting the wing flaps, astronauts control how the Space Shuttle flies.

Fuel
The Space Shuttle's rockets burn liquid hydrogen and oxygen.

Cargo Bay
The cargo bay has a robotic arm that can lift satellites and place them in orbit.

Flight Deck
This is where astronauts fly the Space Shuttle. Both a pilot and a commander sit on the flight deck.

Exercise
Astronauts must exercise every day when they are in space. If they don't, the low gravity will weaken their bones and muscles.

Find Out More on page 29

19

Space Mission

Astronauts go into space for many reasons. Sometimes they fix satellites. Sometimes they spend weeks on a space station, performing experiments and learning. They have to fly on a spacecraft like the Space Shuttle to get into space.

Search & find the following items.

Support Struts

These structures hold a spacecraft together and keep it strong.

Pilot

This member of the crew is in charge of flying the spacecraft.

Engineer

Engineers help maintain all of the equipment the astronauts use during their journey.

Rocket

Rockets propel spacecraft into orbit. They sometimes burn oxygen and hydrogen. They are very powerful.

Rocket Nozzle

The gas produced by the rocket engine is accelerated by the nozzle to very high speeds, producing enough thrust to lift the spacecraft off the ground.

Living Quarters

On any space mission, astronauts eat and sleep in the living quarters of the spacecraft.

Nose Cone

This is the last stage of a rocket, and it is the one that enters orbit. It can contain astronauts and equipment.

Find Out More on page 30

21

Space Station

A space station is a large, man-made structure in orbit around Earth where astronauts can live and work. The newest space station is the International Space Station, and it has been operational since 2000. The astronauts aboard a space station conduct experiments to learn more about medicine, biology, and physics. They can live on the space station for months at a time.

Zero Gravity

Gravity is very low in outer space. Astronauts don't have to walk between modules; they can float!

Search & find the following items.

Space Shuttle

The Space Shuttle carries supplies to the International Space Station.

Solar Array

Collections of solar panels provide electricity for the space station.

Scientist

Astronauts who are scientists perform experiments. They make discoveries about medicine, technology, and more.

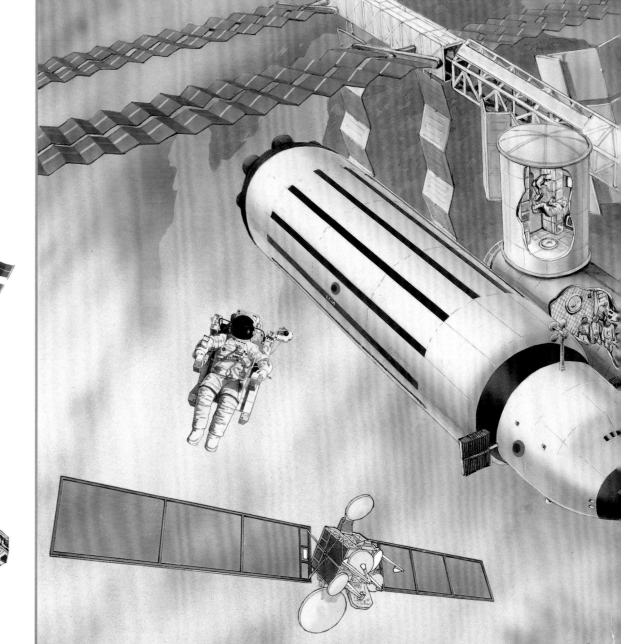

Research

Astronauts on the space station work to figure out how low gravity affects plants and animals.

Docking

When spacecraft fly to the space station, they connect to it so the astronauts can board their new home.

Space Suit

Astronauts wear these suits when outside their spacecraft to control pressure, temperature, oxygen, and radiation.

Satellite

Astronauts sometimes put on space suits and leave the space station to repair satellites.

Find Out More
on page 30

23

24

Mars Mission

Human beings have wanted to go to Mars for a long time. But it's far away and doesn't have any food or water. If people do visit Mars, they will have to plan. What might a mission to Mars look like?

Search & find the following items.

Rock Pick
This tool lets astronauts break off part of a rock and take it back to a lab for study.

Greenhouse
If astronauts stay on Mars for a long time, they will have to grow their own food. A greenhouse lets plants grow in dangerous places.

Dust Devil
Dust devils are giant tornadoes that can be miles high.

Low Gravity
Mars has weaker gravity than Earth does. Astronauts will be able to jump very high.

Mars Land Rover
This will allow astronauts to travel great distances without getting tired.

Canyon
Mars has some very large canyons. One of them is four times as deep as the Grand Canyon.

Hatch Opening
Astronauts move between different parts of a base by traveling through hatches.

Parachute
When a spacecraft lands on Mars, it might use a parachute to slow down.

Space Suit
Astronauts will need space suits to survive on Mars. The air is very thin, and Mars is very cold.

Find Out More
on page 31

Find Out More

Night Sky

It may seem like it's impossible to count all the stars in the sky, but actually astronomers estimate that, on a clear, dark night, a person can see about six thousand stars.

It's easier to see stars when you are in a rural area. City lights are so bright that they wash out the faint starlight.

The brightest star in the sky is Sirius. It is also called the Dog Star.

Every year in July, there is a meteor shower called the Perseids. (It has that name because the meteors appear to come from the constellation Perseus.) During its peak, you can see about sixty meteors per hour.

Did you know that, because of gravity, the same side of the Moon always faces the Earth?

As a comet nears a star, it starts to melt. The tail you see is just that melted ice drifting away from the comet.

Galaxies and Stars

Our Milky Way Galaxy is 100,000 light-years across. One light-year is the distance light travels in one year (around six trillion miles).

Other kinds of galaxies are elliptical galaxies (which are shaped like blobs) and barred spiral galaxies (which look like spiral galaxies, except that they have a straight, bar-shaped part in the center).

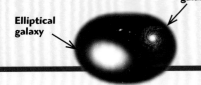

Elliptical galaxy

Spiral galaxy

A binary star is actually two stars that are very close to each other. If one of the stars is more massive than the other, its gravity can pull gas away from the other star.

Nothing can escape a black hole's gravitational pull, not even light.

A supernova is so bright that it can outshine an entire galaxy.

A red giant is an old star whose outer layers of gas have expanded. It is colder than younger stars.

Solar System

For many years, we thought there were nine planets. But recently astronomers began to discover icy bodies past Pluto's orbit, and they noticed that those bodies—Eris and Haumea, among others—were at least the same size as Pluto.

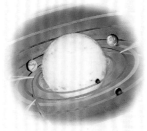

Scientists began to wonder how many other icy bodies were out there, and if they were the same size as Pluto, shouldn't they all be called planets? Eventually the astronomers

had a meeting and decided that Pluto shouldn't be called a planet anymore. Instead, it and the other icy objects are called dwarf planets.

Our own solar system is in an arm of the Milky Way galaxy.

A huge storm called the Great Red Spot has been active on Jupiter for hundreds of years. You can see it through a telescope!

Jupiter

Planets and Moons

Europa fascinates astronomers because it is one of the few places in our solar system that may have life.

Scientists have found that an ocean of liquid water exists far beneath Europa's icy surface, and water is one of the ingredients of life. The ocean is kept liquid by heat created when Jupiter's gravity bends and flexes the moon. Europa's thick surface ice has deep cracks and line patterns from all that stretching.

Mercury and Venus are the only planets in our solar system without moons.

Mars's moon Deimos is our solar system's smallest moon. It's only 7 miles in diameter.

Jupiter has the most moons of any planet in our solar system—more than fifty!

Space Landscapes

Io's surface has a lot of sulfur; that's why it has a splotchy yellow and orange look. It's also the most volcanically active body in the solar system.

Miranda's cliffs are very high. If you dropped a rock from the top of the highest cliff, it would take ten minutes to hit the ground.

Although the Moon looks white, it's actually dark gray. But when viewed against the blackness of space, the gray looks lighter than it really is.

Titan has lakes, but they're not made of water. Instead, they're made of liquid methane.

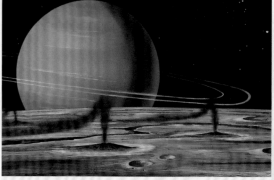

Spacecraft

Even though Voyagers 1 and 2 have left our solar system, they are still transmitting signals to Earth.

Both Voyager spacecraft have special cargo: golden records that contain sounds and images representing life on Earth. The sounds include thunder, birdsong, and human speech. The images include trees, seashells, and people.

The Hubble Space Telescope is as long as a school bus.

When the Hubble Telescope was first launched, it had a slight flaw that produced fuzzy pictures. Astronauts later corrected the problem.

Men first walked on the Moon in 1969. They flew there in the Apollo 11 spacecraft.

Space Shuttle

Before each launch, the Space Shuttle has to be attached to its booster rockets. This process happens inside the Vehicle Assembly Building, the largest single-story building in the world.

When it's ready, the Space Shuttle is moved to the launch site on the Crawler-Transporter. This huge vehicle moves at only 1 mile per hour!

Special tiles on the underside of the Space Shuttle protect it from the intense heat generated when it enters Earth's atmosphere for a landing.

The Space Shuttle program ended on July 21, 2011, when *Atlantis* arrived home from space.

Space Mission

The most powerful rocket ever made was the Saturn V. It stood more than 300 feet tall, taller than the Statue of Liberty!

The Saturn V was the rocket that launched the Apollo 11 mission, taking astronauts to the Moon. It was immensely powerful; in fact, it created more power than eighty-five Hoover Dams.

There are currently at least twenty-five unmanned NASA space missions.

Space Station

The first space station was called Skylab.

Astronauts from the United States, Japan, Russia, Europe, and Canada use the International Space Station. The crew can have as many as six people.

The ISS hovers about 240 miles above the surface of the Earth.

Scientists perform science experiments when they are in the ISS. They try to learn about the origin of the universe and about many other things, such as wether low gravity affects how plants grow.

The space station has many compartments linked together. Some of them are for eating, some for sleeping, and some for conducting science experiments.

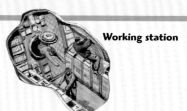

Working station

Exercise station

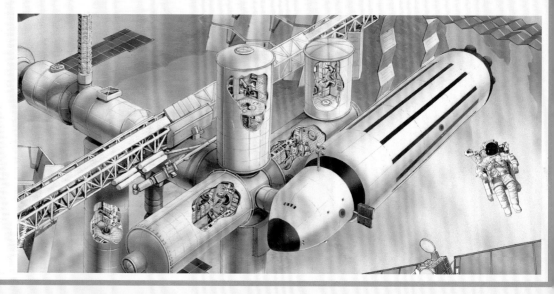

Mars Mission

Mars is about 140 million miles away from Earth. To get to Mars, astronauts would have to travel for seven months.

Mars has the tallest mountain in the solar system, Olympus Mons. It's 14 miles high—three times as high as Mount Everest!

Mars also has a very large canyon called Valles Marineris. It is 2,500 miles long.

Scientists believe that Mars once had life. Recent unmanned missions to Mars have tried to find evidence of water, one of life's building blocks. Mars rovers have tested the Martian soil and seem to have found that evidence.

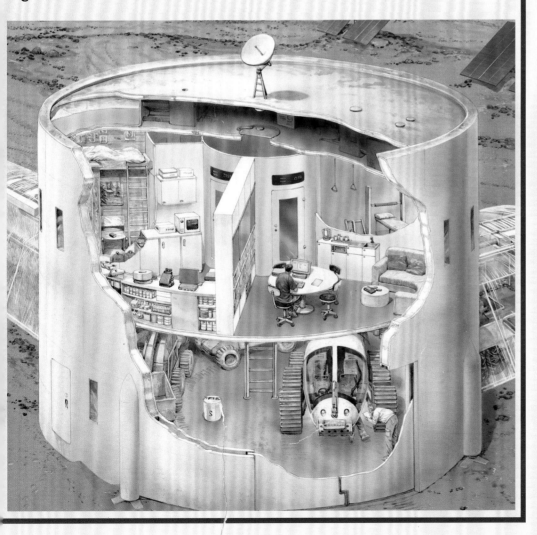